1. Mount Kenya National Park
2. Amboseli National Park
3. Lake Bogoria National Reserve
4. Lake Nakuru National Park
5. Kora National Reserve
6. Tsavo National Park
7. Masai Mara National Preserve
8. Arusha National Park
9. Serengeti National Park
10. Ngorongoro Crater Conservation Area
11. Mount Kilimanjaro National Park
12. Tarangire National Park
13. Lake Manyara National Park
14. Mabamba Swamps
15. Murchison Falls National Park
16. Budongo Forest
17. Kibale Forest National Park
18. Queen Elizabeth National Park
19. Lake Mburo National Park
20. Gombe National Park
21. Ruaha National Park
22. Katavi National Park
23. Mikumi National Park
24. Udzungwa National Park

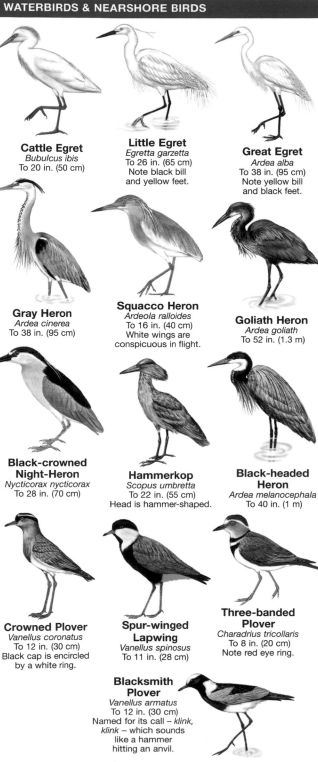

A POCKET NATURALIST® GUIDE

EAST AFRICA BIRDS

A Folding Pocket Guide to Familiar Species in Kenya, Tanzania & Uganda

EAST AFRICA BIRDS – A Folding Pocket Guide to Familiar Species

WATERFORD PRESS

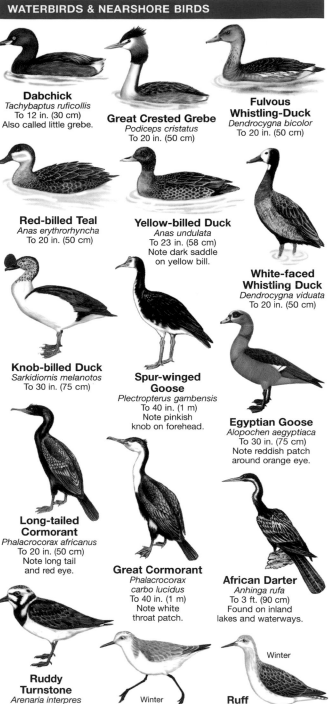

Dabchick
Tachybaptus ruficollis
To 12 in. (30 cm)
Also called little grebe.

Great Crested Grebe
Podiceps cristatus
To 20 in. (50 cm)

Fulvous Whistling-Duck
Dendrocygna bicolor
To 20 in. (50 cm)

Red-billed Teal
Anas erythrorhyncha
To 20 in. (50 cm)

Yellow-billed Duck
Anas undulata
To 23 in. (58 cm)
Note dark saddle on yellow bill.

White-faced Whistling Duck
Dendrocygna viduata
To 20 in. (50 cm)

Knob-billed Duck
Sarkidiornis melanotos
To 30 in. (75 cm)

Spur-winged Goose
Plectropterus gambensis
To 40 in. (1 m)
Note pinkish knob on forehead.

Egyptian Goose
Alopochen aegyptiaca
To 30 in. (75 cm)
Note reddish patch around orange eye.

Long-tailed Cormorant
Phalacrocorax africanus
To 20 in. (50 cm)
Note long tail and red eye.

Great Cormorant
Phalacrocorax carbo lucidus
To 40 in. (1 m)
Note white throat patch.

African Darter
Anhinga rufa
To 3 ft. (90 cm)
Found on inland lakes and waterways.

Ruddy Turnstone
Arenaria interpres
To 10 in. (25 cm)

Sanderling
Calidris alba
To 8 in. (20 cm)
Runs in and out with waves along shorelines.
Winter

Ruff
Philomachus pugnax
To 12 in. (30 cm)
Winter

Cattle Egret
Bubulcus ibis
To 20 in. (50 cm)

Little Egret
Egretta garzetta
To 26 in. (65 cm)
Note black bill and yellow feet.

Great Egret
Ardea alba
To 38 in. (95 cm)
Note yellow bill and black feet.

Gray Heron
Ardea cinerea
To 38 in. (95 cm)

Squacco Heron
Ardeola ralloides
To 16 in. (40 cm)
White wings are conspicuous in flight.

Goliath Heron
Ardea goliath
To 52 in. (1.3 m)

Black-crowned Night-Heron
Nycticorax nycticorax
To 28 in. (70 cm)

Hammerkop
Scopus umbretta
To 22 in. (55 cm)
Head is hammer-shaped.

Black-headed Heron
Ardea melanocephala
To 40 in. (1 m)

Crowned Plover
Vanellus coronatus
To 12 in. (30 cm)
Black cap is encircled by a white ring.

Spur-winged Lapwing
Vanellus spinosus
To 11 in. (28 cm)

Three-banded Plover
Charadrius tricollaris
To 8 in. (20 cm)
Note red eye ring.

Blacksmith Plover
Vanellus armatus
To 12 in. (30 cm)
Named for its call – klink, klink – which sounds like a hammer hitting an anvil.

Hadada Ibis
Bostrychia hagedash
To 3 ft. (90 cm)
Note red mark on bill and white facial crescent. Call is a loud – ha-de-dah.

Lesser Flamingo
Phoeniconaias minor
To 40 in. (1 m)
The larger greater flamingo has a pinker bill.

Shoebill
Balaeniceps rex
To 4 ft. (1.2 m)
Inhabits swamps of east and central Africa.

Sacred Ibis
Threskiornis aethiopica
To 3 ft. (90 cm)

African Spoonbill
Platalea alba
To 3 ft. (90 cm)
Bill has a spoon-shaped tip.

Marabou Stork
Leptoptilos crumeniferus
To 5 ft. (1.5 m)
Scavenger competes with vultures for carrion.

Glossy Ibis
Plegadis falcinellus
To 26 in. (65 cm)

Saddle-billed Stork
Ephippiorhynchus senegalensis
To 5 ft. (1.5 m)
Bill has a yellow saddle. East Africa's largest stork.

Black-winged Stilt
Himantopus himantopus
To 15 in. (38 cm)

White Stork
Ciconia ciconia
To 4 ft. (1.2 m)

Yellow-billed Stork
Mycteria ibis
To 40 in. (1 m)

Gray-crowned Crane
Balearica regulorum
To 42 in. (1.1 m)
National Bird of Tanzania and Uganda.

Pied Avocet
Recurvirostra avosetta
To 18 in. (45 cm)

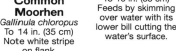

Black Crake
Amaurornis flavirostris
To 8 in. (20 cm)
Note red legs and yellow bill.

Caspian Tern
Hydroprogne caspia
To 2 ft. (60 cm)

African Jacana
Actophilornis africana
To 12 in. (30 cm)
Long-toed swamp bird walks on the floating leaves of aquatic plants.

Common Moorhen
Gallinula chloropus
To 14 in. (35 cm)
Note white stripe on flank.

African Skimmer
Rynchops flavirostris
To 15 in. (38 cm)
Feeds by skimming over water with its lower bill cutting the water's surface.

Red-knobbed Coot
Fulica cristata
To 18 in. (45 cm)
2 red forehead knobs are prominent during breeding season.

Gray-headed Gull
Chroicocephalus cirrocephalus
To 16 in. (40 cm)

Great White Pelican
Pelecanus onocrotalus
To 5.5 ft. (1.7 m)
The similar pink-backed pelican is smaller and has a pinkish bill.

OSTRICH, ETC.

Helmeted Guineafowl
Numida meleagris
To 22 in. (55 cm)

Red-necked Francolin
Francolinus afer
To 14 in. (35 cm)
Note red on throat and face.

Kori Bustard
Choriotis kori
To 52 in. (1.3 m)
One of the world's heaviest flying birds. The smaller black bustard has a black head, neck and undersides and a white ear patch.

Ostrich
Struthio spp.
To 9 ft. (2.7 m)
The largest and heaviest bird on earth.

BIRDS OF PREY & VULTURES

Bateleur
Terathopius ecaudatus
To 2 ft. (60 cm)
Note short tail.
Underwings are white
with a black
trailing edge.

Martial Eagle
Polemaetus bellicosus
To 32 in. (80 cm)

Tawny Eagle
Aquila rapax
To 30 in. (75 cm)
Plumage on legs and
underparts is shaggy.

Black Eagle
Aquila verreauxii
To 32 in. (80 cm)
Has a white V-shaped
line on its back.

African Fish-Eagle
Haliaeetus vocifer
To 32 in. (80 cm)

Crowned Eagle
Spizaetus coronatus
To 5 ft. (1.5 m)
Note head crest.
Africa's largest eagle.

Black Kite
Milvus migrans
To 22 in. (55 cm)
Several variants exist.
Notched tail is key
field mark.

African Hawk Eagle
Hieraaetus spilogaster
To 26 in. (65 cm)
White breast is
heavily streaked.

Long-crested Eagle
Lophaetus occipitalis
To 22 in. (55 cm)

Black-shouldered Kite
Elanus caeruleus
To 14 in. (35 cm)
Note all-white tail.

Common Kestrel
Falco tinnunculus
To 12 in. (30 cm)

Lanner Falcon
Falco biarmicus
To 18 in. (45 cm)
Note reddish
crown.

Osprey
Pandion haliaetus
To 2 ft. (60 cm)
Fish-eating raptor.

Augur Buzzard
Buteo augur
To 52 in. (1.3 m)
Note reddish tail.

BIRDS OF PREY & VULTURES

Giant Eagle-Owl
Bubo lacteus
To 26 in. (65 cm)
Call is a pig-
like grunt.

African Scops Owl
Otus senegalensis
To 8 in. (20 cm)

Hooded Vulture
Necrosyrtes monachus
To 30 in. (75 cm)

White-headed Vulture
Aegypius occipitalis
To 32 in. (80 cm)
Note red and blue bill.

Egyptian Vulture
Neophron percnopterus
To 26 in. (65 cm)
Tool-using bird breaks open
ostrich eggs with rocks.

White-backed Vulture
Gyps africanus
To 38 in. (95 cm)

Lappet-faced Vulture
Torgos tracheliotus
To 40 in. (1 m)
Heavy-billed vulture
dominates other birds
at animal carcasses.

Secretarybird
Sagittarius serpentarius
To 52 in. (1.3 m)
Hunts along the ground
and often kills prey by
stomping it with its feet.

DOVES, KINGFISHERS, ETC.

Ring-necked Dove
Streptopelia capicola
To 12 in. (30 cm)
Call is a continuous –
work-HARD-er.

Speckled Pigeon
Columba guinea
To 12 in. (30 cm)

White-bellied Go-Away-Bird
Corythaixoides leucogaster
To 20 in. (50 cm)
Named for its sheep-like
bleating call – go-wayeer.

Laughing Dove
Streptopelia senegalensis
To 10 in. (25 cm)
Note spots on neck.

Chestnut-bellied Sandgrouse
Pterocles exustus
To 12 in.

Namaqua Dove
Oena capensis
To 12 in. (30 cm)
Note long tail.

DOVES, KINGFISHERS, ETC.

Giant Kingfisher
Megaceryle maxima
To 19 in. (48 cm)

Pied Kingfisher
Ceryle rudis
To 10 in. (25 cm)

Striped Kingfisher
Halcyon chelicuti
To 7 in. (18 cm)

Woodland Kingfisher
Halcyon senegalensis
To 9 in. (23 cm)

Malachite Kingfisher
Alcedo cristata
To 6 in. (15 cm)

Crested Hoopoe
Upupa epops
To 12 in. (30 cm)
Head crest is erect when
alarmed. Call is a soft
repeated – hoop-hoop.

White-browed Coucal
Centropus superciliosus
To 15 in. (38 cm)

Alpine Swift
Tachymarptis melba
To 9 in. (23 cm)

Speckled Mousebird
Colius striatus
To 14 in. (35 cm)
Bill is black above,
white below.

Diederik Cuckoo
Chrysococcyx caprius
To 7 in. (18 cm)
Call is a clear –
dee-dee-deederik.

Brown Parrot
Poicephalus meyeri
To 10 in. (25 cm)

Green Wood Hoopoe
Phoeniculus purpureus
To 15 in. (38 cm)
Travels in small flocks
through savanna
woodlands.

Fischer's Lovebird
Agapornis fischeri
To 6 in. (15 cm)

Lilac-breasted Roller
Coracias caudata
To 15 in. (38 cm)
National Bird
of Kenya.

HORNBILLS, BEE-EATERS, ETC.

European Bee-Eater
Merops apiaster
To 11 in. (28 cm)

Carmine Bee-eater
Merops nubicus
To 15 in. (38 cm)

Little Bee-eater
Merops pusillus
To 6 in. (15 cm)

Red-billed Hornbill
Tockus erythrorhynchus
To 18 in. (45 cm)

Yellow-billed Hornbill
Tockus flavirostris
To 18 in. (45 cm)

Southern Ground Hornbill
Bucorvus leadbeateri
To 42 in. (1.1 m)

Red & Yellow Barbet
Trachyphonus erythrocephalus
To 9 in. (23 cm)

Greater Honeyguide
Indicator indicator
To 8 in. (20 cm)
Guides humans and other
mammals to bee nests.

PERCHING BIRDS

Lesser Striped Swallow
Hirundo abyssinica
To 6 in. (15 cm)
Underparts are
heavily streaked.

Common Waxbill
Estrilda astrild
To 5 in. (13 cm)

Yellow Wagtail
Motacilla flava
To 6 in. (15 cm)
Head may be black, gray
or yellow. Wags tail when
foraging on the ground.

White-browed Robin Chat
Cossypha heuglini
To 8 in. (20 cm)

Common Wattle-eye
Platysteira cyanea
To 5 in. (13 cm)

African Pied Wagtail
Motacilla aguimp
To 8 in. (20 cm)

PERCHING BIRDS

Stonechat
Saxicola torquatus
To 5 in. (13 cm)

Common Bulbul
Pycnonotus barbatus
To 9 in. (23 cm)
Note yellow undertail
feathers. Very common.

Rufous-naped Lark
Mirafra africana
To 7 in. (18 cm)
Call is a mournful –
tseep-tseeoo.

African Paradise-Flycatcher
Terpsiphone viridis
To 14 in. (35 cm)

Gray-headed Bush Shrike
Malaconotus blanchoti
To 10 in. (25 cm)
Call is a mournful –
hoooooooooooo.

Common Fiscal Shrike
Lanius collaris
To 9 in. (23 cm)
Wing bars form a white
'V' on its back when
perching. Also called
butcherbird.

Chinspot Batis
Batis molitor
To 5 in. (13 cm)
Females have a
chestnut breast band
and chin patch.

African Yellow White-eye
Zosterops senegalensis
To 4 in. (10 cm)

Red-billed Quelea
Quelea quelea
To 5 in. (13 cm)
Note red bill and
black mask. One of
the most abundant
African birds.

Scarlet-chested Sunbird
Nectarinia senegalensis
To 6 in. (15 cm)

Collared Sunbird
Anthreptes collaris
To 4 in. (10 cm)

Malachite Sunbird
Nectarinia famosa
To 10 in. (25 cm)

Yellow-fronted Canary
Serinus mozambicus
To 5 in. (13 cm)

Red-billed Firefinch
Lagonosticta senegala
To 4 in. (10 cm)
The only firefinch
with a red bill.

Yellow-bellied Sunbird
Cinnyris venustus
To 4 in. (10 cm)

PERCHING BIRDS

Pin-tailed Whydah
Vidua macroura
To 12 in. (30 cm)

Red-cheeked Cordonbleu
Uraeginthus bengalus
To 5 in. (13 cm)

Red-headed Weaver
Anaplectes rubriceps
To 6 in. (15 cm)
Weavers create pendulous
nests that dangle from
tree branches.

Black-headed Weaver
Ploceus cucullatus
To 6 in. (15 cm)

Masked Weaver
Ploceus velatus
To 6 in. (15 cm)

Red Bishop
Euplectes orix
To 5 in. (13 cm)
The similar golden
bishop has black and
yellow plumage.

Yellow-billed Oxpecker
Buphagus africanus
To 9 in. (23 cm)
Feeds on the parasites of
large grazing mammals.

Golden-breasted Starling
Cosmopsarus regius
To 14 in. (35 cm)

Superb Starling
Spreo superbus
To 7 in. (18 cm)

Red-winged Starling
Onycognathus morio
To 11 in. (28 cm)
Chestnut primaries
are conspicuous
in flight.

White-necked Raven
Corvus albicollis
To 22 in. (55 cm)
Note massive
white-tipped bill.

African Drongo
Dicrurus adsimilis
To 10 in. (25 cm)
Note forked tail.

Pied Crow
Corvus albus
To 20 in. (50 cm)

Wattled Starling
Creatophora cinerea
To 9 in. (23 cm)